Remember LEE

THE END IS THE BEGINNING

A mother's journey through loss

By Linda Leith Musser
Design and Illustration By Ron Boldt

©Copyright 1991
God is a Birdwatcher
Revised 1998
The End is the Beginning
Centering Corporation
All rights reserved

ISBN#1-56123-020-0
SAN#298-1815

Additional copies may be ordered from:

A Centering Corporation Resource
1531 N. Saddle Creek Rd.
Omaha, NE 68104
Phone: 402-553-1200/Fax: 402-553-0507
Email: J1200@AOL.com

A Note from Linda

I didn't start out to write a book or an article or a story. I'm not a diary keeper or a journal writer. I'm a very private person with a horror of letting too many people into the real me.

I wrote because I hurt. I wrote because at times writing was the only way I was able to get some of the pain out. It has been a way to express feelings without hurting anyone else, a way to clarify my thinking to myself.

I have no illusions that what I have written is an answer for anyone else's grief. I don't pretend to have unraveled the mystery of death or the experience of mourning. I believe that it is very likely that I have not finished my own process.

I have lost my son – a handsome, lovable young man, who died when he was 18 years old. It is a loss that continues and will continue for the rest of my life. I will always miss him – the person who was and the person who might have been. There will always be questions of: I wonder if Lee had lived, if...They will remain unanswered.

There are other questions, too. Why did it happen? To him? To me? What vicious bad luck or fate caused it? Why? I don't know. I never will.

I have learned from it and maybe that is why it's important for me to share it. I have learned that people are kinder than I ever believed. I have learned that looking at one's self is one of the most difficult things to do. I have learned to believe that God does more than just watch sparrows. I have learned that grief is, even when shared, an intensely lonely experience. It is something you do alone, even in a room full of people, a private agony.

There were times when I felt no one cared, even though I knew many did. There were times when I mistrusted those I trust the most. There were times when I hid the truth and the pain from others who would have helped, even when I needed the help. In most ways, I'm just like others who grieve. This is just one person's record of a very difficult journey.

The End is the Beginning

∙∙

The nurse comes around the corner with a clipboard in her hand. She seems rushed and I have a sense of being a bother to her. I ask, "How is he? What is his condition?"

"At this point he is very critical…we're working to get some vital signs." Deep down in my gut I know he is dead, but I keep up the charade.
"Was he drinking?"
"I don't know. He was with friends."
"Does he have any allergies?"
"No."
"Does he have seizures?"
"No."
"Is he diabetic?"
"No. He's the world's healthiest kid."
"We're just trying to find out what could have happened. I'll get back to you and let you know any information." Arm squeeze. She is gone. I never see her again.

I'm a nurse. I have been for 19 years. I always thought most nurses were helpful, caring people who recognized family needs. All I asked for was to know if he was alive and what was being done. I felt I was a bother to her, a hysterical mother stereotype. My son died at the end of her shift and probably caused her to be late getting home. Her charting probably lasted longer than it should have. The room needed to be cleaned up. She was late. She made me feel I ought to apologize for disturbing her, should be instructing my children not to get killed while she's on duty. I wanted to slap some caring into her and force her to give more than lip service to the idea, but I couldn't, because as she went back to the room, she might be the one who brings my son back. Such incredible power she has. She is invulnerable to me. I wonder if she has any idea what it's like.

April 20th

....

It is 4:30 a.m. I wake up and walk to the kitchen, knowing that I am awake to stay. The thought that Lee is dead is unreal and yet I believe it. I am amazed at the sensation of numbness I feel. One's mind can certainly anesthetize itself. I am clear-headed, tearless and functioning. At the same time, I am numb and shaking. I sit at the kitchen table, coffee brewing, and think of what I need to do. There is a pad of paper and a pencil on the table. I am not consciously thinking. It's almost a trance-like feeling, too calm, too controlled, too numb.

I pick up the pencil and suddenly I'm writing. There is no plan, just words pushing onto the paper. I don't stop or think or cross out or rewrite. It's just there, almost as if it wrote itself. I reread it and am satisfied. I call Lee's favorite teacher and ask if he will read it at the funeral. He says he will be glad to. I want desperately to say it myself, but I'm afraid. It says what I want to say about Lee. I don't trust anyone else to know what to say. I will not let Lee's funeral be one suited to anyone else. It must be special, it must be him. Later, I will take what I've written to the funeral home. The funeral director will make 400 copies of it, and they will all be gone.

By noon I am at the mall with my daughter, Michelle, waiting to get haircuts. We somehow feel the need to look presentable at the funeral home. We are done at different times, so I walk to the drugstore to buy some stockings while Michelle is finishing.

Ahead of me I see Betty. She used to work with me. She is a good natured, gossipy, larger-than-life character; too loud, too noisy at times. I have no desire to see her, so I cross to the other side of the mall walkway to avoid her. I am leaden. It's difficult to walk. I don't want to talk to her, but she is coming across the aisle, flapping arms and packages and shrieking, "Linda! Good to see you!" I can think of no escape. I can find no way to run. She rattles on and on and I just stand there. Finally she says, "How's your family?" I look at her. "My son was killed Saturday night. I'm on my way home to get ready to go to the funeral home."

It's as though someone stuck a pin in her. She deflates and says, "Oh, my God. I'm so sorry." I feel sorry for her. I probably should have said nothing and spared her this awkwardness. I say I have to leave and walk away. She is still standing in the same place when I turn the corner into the beauty shop.

Before we leave, I remember the guys, pallbearers now. They've been such a part of our lives, like six or seven sons. I want to do something. I want them to have a tangible remembrance. I talk to Michelle. We go to a little jewelry store and pick out key rings with an oval medallion made of pewter. Michelle suggests we have them engraved with the word, *Friends,* so we do.

The obituary is in the paper. There is a heading, *Man Killed In Accident.* The phone rings and a young man's voice says, "Hello. Is Lee home?" and laughs. I hang up and stand in the kitchen staring at the phone. I am violently nauseated and shaking. I pray he doesn't call when one of the kids answers the phone.

• •

Arrangements

I am afraid there won't be any people there.
I am afraid there won't be any flowers.
I want the world to stop and notice my son is dead.
I want everyone to suffer and grieve.
I want everyone to know that we love him
and our world will never be the same without him.

The funeral director asks me if the room is too big.
I'm afraid it is.
I don't want it to be empty.
He asks me how many people will be there.
I have no idea. Maybe a hundred?
He suggests we leave the room undivided
and close it off later if necessary.
I agree.

· ·

The Visitation

I walk to the door of the room. It is huge, empty rows of folding chairs waiting. Silence. There are eight gold and crystal chandeliers. Sofas and chairs are spaced around the room, soft colors, pinkish light from lamps. It is a room at odds with itself, trying to give a homey appearance to a cavern, partially elegant around the edges, collapsibly utilitarian in the center. Forgettable music is playing from somewhere.

There is a stand at the door holding a pen, an empty guest book, a small light. There are beautiful live plants scattered on tables; some, too large, fill corners of the room. I wonder how they can live where there are no windows. It takes me a long time to realize the plants have been sent to us. I look to the front of the room. There is a wall, probably 100 feet long, filled with flower arrangements. I am stunned. I had no idea there would be so many. They are exquisite and wasteful, beautiful and temporary. It's odd. I don't smell any flowers. Even more bizarre, I have a sudden image, Rose Bowl Parade of Death.

In the center of all the flowers is the casket—purple mums and carnations—school colors. Lee is lying there. He looks as though he is sleeping, unmarked, unmoving; blue blazer, beige and blue shirt, beige slacks and tie. He is handsome, even in death. They have done their job well.

I try to help those in the family who are seeing him for the first time. The funeral director asks if we are ready. There are people waiting outside. I say "Yes, I guess so." How does one get ready for this? People are walking in, talking softly. The ritual begins.

I am standing next to Lee. My mother-in-law walks up and introduces me to an older lady, a friend of hers from church. The woman glances down at Lee, lying in the casket, and says, "What happened? Break his neck?"

There is a reflex jerk of my arm. It dawns on me that I am, in a split second, going to slap this woman in the face. I stop my arm from moving. I stare at her and say nothing. I could, at this moment, kill her. Then at her funeral I would walk up to her daughter and say, "What happened? Break her neck?"

An eye for an eye.

They are sitting in rows, quiet, solemn. It is not in keeping with their youth. They have on suits and ties or dresses. They look awkward, uncomfortable and beautiful. Some are silent, others crying, row after row of chairs filled with classmates and friends. Several sit with bowed heads. Lee's closest friends have been here the entire time; in a sense, hosts for their peers. Ownership of grief acknowledged. I see Mike, head down, hands covering his eyes. Jeff, more verbal, is surrounded by boys in the lobby.

Faces I have never seen come forward and seek from me some comfort. I am suddenly mother to all of them, somehow wanting to protect them all. Some are emotional, sobbing and tearful, holding me and yet somehow ending up being held. Some stilted words, carefully rehearsed: "I would like to convey my deepest expression of sympathy on your loss," from a 16 year old! Some try to get words out and fail. For them, I try to cover, helping them through the ritual. One girl asks if she and I can pray and stands expectantly watching me. I suddenly realize she is waiting for me to pray and I search for words, unable to put any together. A few sentences and she is gone, returning time after time to hug me.

There are young men, some trying desperately to remain in control, others sobbing unashamedly as they talk. They talk about laughing with Lee, about jokes and stunts and memories. They share pieces of Lee with me; Lee the friend, not Lee the son.

There is an endless line of them down this huge room and out the door. It is the ultimate contradiction, youth and death. They leave tokens. One boy asks if it's all right if he puts a St. Christopher medal in the casket. I find a picture of a pretty girl with a message on the back, "To my good friend, Lee. Love Chris." It is carefully tucked in the corner of the casket near his head. There are notes in round, large handwriting. I put them in his pocket.

They each want to do and say the right thing. I'm sure that for many of them, this is their first experience with death. I feel responsible for them all.

Many of them tell me what classes they were in with Lee and how they knew him. Many tell me that he helped them, with algebra, with computers. One tells me how he helped by being a friend when her parents were divorcing.

The school guidance counselor stops and says she has had a steady parade of them in her office, asking what to wear, what to say. They keep coming up and hugging me. I am trying very hard to give them each something. They can't possibly know what they are giving me.

The adults are different. Some look awkward, shaking their heads, wordless. Some say things like, " You have my sympathy," and I wonder what that means. People I haven't seen for years, old co-workers, classmates, make me realize how fragile relationships are. I am grateful they cared enough to come. I am amazed that some of them even remember me.

People I don't know introduce themselves, tell who they are. I am astounded by how many people knew Lee. People I don't know. There are neighbors whose kids grew up with mine, sobbing. "I should be comforting you, and look at me," then stumbling away. I see Lee's boss, crying loudly, hushed by counter girls from Kentucky Fried Chicken where he worked.

A man my husband Ted works with grabs me in a bear hug, hoarse voice in my ear, "Son of a Bitch!" he says, and disappears. My good friend, Mary, holding me, hugging me, saying nothing, eyes meet, we share. I want her near me. I keep spotting her, pulling some-thing from her presence.

I am hugged, kissed and patted. I am consumed by all these peo-ple. I keep seeing this line of faces, snaking out of the room. Ted is next to me, my young son, Curt, is near me, Michelle is standing by. Each of us talking to these people.

I had no idea there would be so many. I am exhausted and thirsty. I cannot sit down. I stand for hours and cannot, will not, go to the other room and "rest."

Curt counts the names in the visitor's book — 750. There are 50 floral arrangements. I had no idea so many people would care.

The adults have learned. They know the customs. Most of them speak briefly and move on, but the kids give you their guts, not yet having perfected the veneer. They share real feelings, real pain, real emotion. It is exhausting and caring. It is painful and comforting. It is wrenching and helpful. I love them for it and yet I wish I could save them from it.

The Funeral

● ●

It is a gorgeous, sunny Spring day. I am wearing a white suit. I refuse to allow myself to wear the black one. The flowers are beginning to look faded. The pallbearers are gathered. I've never seen them in suits before. Suddenly, they seem like strangers, tall, young men in navy blue. I hope none of them had to go buy a suit. I hadn't thought of that before. They have on boutonnieres. They should be going to a dance. Each one hugs me.

There is a young man standing by the door. I've never him seen before. He has on a black jacket, dress shirt and tie. He is sniffling and I realize he is crying. I look at him and he shakes his head slowly and looks embarrassed. He walks forward, with his head down, not meeting my eyes and says, "I'm sorry, but is there anyone I can ride with to the cemetery? I didn't have a ride here. I used to talk to Lee at work. I walked from Crown Point, left my house at 7 this morning. I couldn't not be here, but I don't have a ride to the cemetery. I'll walk home afterwards," tears sliding down his cheeks.

I walk to the office of the funeral director and I tell, not ask, *tell,* them to find him a ride. I don't care if he has to ride with the minister or if he rides in a limousine. This young man who walked seven miles to be at Lee's funeral *will* get where he wants to go.

I see him later at the cemetery. I hear afterwards that one of the guys took him home. I never found out his name, but I'll always love him.

The band is setting up quietly, dressed in their black concert uniforms. There are 80 of them, silent. I called the band director on Monday and asked if there might be one or two members of the band who could play something at the funeral. She said she would see, and asked me how large the room was at the funeral home. I had no idea. She said she would take care of it. I found out that the entire band had volunteered to play. There are two school buses, a van, 80 instruments and 80 band members here. They are hushed and intent on their task of setting up, trying not to let tubas and music stands rattle. They are to be seated, 40 on each side of the room, facing Lee's casket.

People keep coming in. Ted and I walk to our seats, Michelle and Curt between us. As I'm walking, I realize there are no empty chairs in the room. I am concentrating on keeping my legs from shaking, afraid I will fall. I don't want this to begin, because in an hour it will be over and Lee will be gone forever. I hear people crying. I am intent on standing up straight, placing one foot in front of the other, this simple task suddenly overwhelming. I make it to the sofa reserved for us. I am safe. My legs can shake now and no one will know.

The minister begins to speak. I have no idea what he is saying. I know words like tragedy and memories and God and love and prayer are said. I am not comforted. I am staring at Lee's profile. I am memorizing his face, his jaw line, his hair. I am not crying. I am desperately trying to burn him into my brain. Time is so short. I need more time to spend with him.

I notice that the band is going to play. The music is muted, dignified, soft. The director has 80 sets of eyes glued to her. She tells them exactly what she wants, with both baton and body. They are perfect. This is the same high school marching band that can raise the roof off the gym and be heard from the football field a mile away, but now they sound almost delicate. It is moving and fitting and beautiful. A blonde girl with a flute is crying.

Lee's teacher, Mr. Williams, comes forward and begins to read the letter I wrote when I couldn't sleep. I hear people sobbing. I have an incredible urge to tell him to go slowly. I want more time. I stare at Lee's hands, his shoulders, his eyebrows.

The minister closes with a prayer and people file past the casket. There are people I don't know, people I see every day, people who have traveled miles. There are hundreds of them. I am astonished. The band files out first, row after row of young people in black. After them, all the others. Some touch his hand. Others nod, as if in greeting. Some are being helped, some are the helpers. They are blocking him. I can't see him. Now I don't want to see him. I know that when I do, it will be for the last time.

There is no one left. Ted and Michelle and Curt and I stand next to him, pat his shoulder, touch his hand, stroke his hair. I'm staring at his face. I have the sensation of being alone with him; that somehow, some way, at this point, it is just the two of us. I reach down and gently loosen his necktie. I hear someone whisper. "What is she doing?" Someone else replies, "I don't know." It doesn't matter. I just know he'd loosen it himself if he could. Then, one last time, I comb my fingers through his hair. Very softly, very quietly, so no one else can hear, for the last time, like I have every night for the last 18 years I whisper, *"Good night, Lee",* and turn and walk away.

The Cemetery

● ●

We are ushered into a room and told to wait. I have no idea why, until it dawns on me that they are closing the casket. Ted's aunt hugs me and whispers, "You're a good mother," and I say, "God knows, I tried."

They tell us to come and we walk like robots to the door, watching the casket go into the hearse. I am suddenly afraid. I don't know if the boys are strong enough. They look thin and vulnerable.

The limo turns into the cemetery and I look back. There is still a line of cars coming. There is a tent and the entire band seated in a semicircle on folding chairs. I didn't know the band was going to the cemetery. I thought they had gone back to school. I wonder where the buses are. I can't see them.

The flowers are neatly arranged in rows, banked in aisles leading to the tent, rows of chairs, casket now in place. We walk and are seated. The sun is brilliant, robins singing, people standing facing us. The pallbearers stand across from us, never meeting my eyes, looking at the casket. The minister talks briefly. He nods and the band begins to play, fuller this time, more outdoor volume permissible. A girl with the clarinet is sobbing and blowing at the same time. A boy with a trumpet has tears sliding down his cheeks.

The minister speaks again, and at a signal from him the pallbearers all take off their boutonnieres and lay them on top of the casket. The wind is blowing and it seems colder. I think it is over and suddenly, from very far to the right, I hear "Taps" from a trumpet. A few seconds later, from far to the left, an echo, then another behind me. I see people turning, looking, trying to see where they are coming from. It is incredibly beautiful, perfect, sad, brassy echoes from different directions, invisible and unreal. They never miss a beat or a note.

Then, it really is over. I walk over to the band and thank them, tell them they will never know how much it meant to us. I turn and see the band director sobbing in her husband's arms. I start to walk to the car and for some reason, look up. At the top of the hill, next to a small tree, backlit by the sun, there are silhouettes of two young men in black, holding trumpets. In my mind, I thank them for what was an incredible performance. I have no idea who they were.

Afterward

• •

We go to the church afterwards for what someone calls a memorial luncheon. There are flowers there, left from the funeral. The room is filled with over a hundred people. All the food people have been bringing to the house is being served. I wonder if it will be enough, not really caring.

I walk around, greeting people again. I find myself being compli-
mented on the beautiful funeral. It's as though I am the director of
a stage play and the reviews are coming in. I feel like an actress,
nodding and smiling and playing a role. I have not cried over the
death of my son.

People keep telling me to eat. I put food on a plate and smear it
around. The prop stops the questions and the urging. I don't eat
any of it.

Snatches of conversation as I move from table to table, hostessing:

He was a fine young man.
It was a beautiful service. I will never forget the trumpets.
Have you ever seen so many flowers?
There were 120 cars in the procession.
How is she doing? We shouldn't leave her alone.
It was very special.
Do you want to go for a ride in my car and scream?
If there's anything I can do. Call me.
What do you want me to do with the rest of the ham?
How are the kids doing?
Where did the band get the black uniforms?
Are you all right?
It was magnificent.

I am hugged and squeezed and given meaningful looks. I am on
stage. I don't sit down, I keep moving, keep talking. There is
enough food for all, with boxes of leftovers going to my house.
People keep touching me.

The funeral director and staff are there. He apologizes for their
presence, saying he hopes they are not an intrusion. They don't
usually attend these things. He looks apologetic and says they did-
n't want to leave because this one was so special. He seems
embarrassed. I guess the play was a hit. The director of many says
it was unique. I feel a sense of accomplishment, some kind of desperate satisfaction, a hideous success. I gave my son a memorable
funeral.

May

I feel like two people; not because I want to be, but because I have to be. One is made of stainless steel – shiny, brittle, hard. She reflects, like a mirror, the appearance of normalcy. She goes to work, interacts with people, helps with homework, and accomplishes all things that need to be done. She cannot be dented or scratched and only shows emotion when others deem it appropriate. She has aching jaws from gritted teeth and a constant pain between her shoulder blades from holding herself erect. Her stomach survives only by the grace of Rolaids, but no one knows because her stainless steel skin shows nothing. She has always been *strong,* therefore, *she will be strong!* She has always been *in control,* therefore, *she will continue to be in control.* She has always been the one others lean on; therefore, she does not allow herself to lean. She is who she is because others expect it and because the only way to deal with pain is to not feel it. The price she pays is to feel nothing. Nothing is funny, nothing is worth anger. There is no joy. Laughter exits the mouth only because it sometimes constitutes appropriate behavior. Ambition is gone and drive and motivation are replaced by apathy. Living in black and white instead of color – everything, shades of grey.

The other person feels. She wants only to crawl into some lonely, dark cave like a wounded animal and moan, bleeding her soul and hopes into the dirt. She watches helplessly as her bones melt and ooze in rivers of white pain, feeling her intestines writhing as razor-cut memories slice off inch after inch. If *she* takes over, the pain will win. It will consume myself and there will be no trace of the me who was, so I fight her. I lock her into a square iron box with heavy hinges that sits inside of me, near where my heart should be. I keep pushing down on the lid of the box, but it keeps pushing open and the pain jumps out and slashes at me. I keep fighting, keep holding, keep squeezing down with all my strength to keep this pain box closed and the horror safely locked inside. I am not strong enough. I am terrified of getting weaker. If I ever let go and let the thing out of the box, it will devour me and I, too, will die.

Mass

●●●

A lady calls and says there is a special service being said for Lee at the Catholic church. I am confused. We aren't Catholic. What is she talking about? She tells me a group of Lee's friends, members of this church, talked to the priest about Lee's death. They wanted to do something, but were concerned because Lee was not Catholic. They were afraid it was not permissible. The priest offered to hold a service. I am amazed. I anticipate a traditional mass with the mention of Lee's name. I am not prepared for what is to come.

When we arrive at the church we are greeted by several of Lee's friends and escorted to reserved pews at the very front. Our seating is followed by a procession: priest, altar boys, candles and music. There are responsive readings led by a teenage girl. People stand and kneel, sit and stand. The priest thoughtfully tells the front rows of non-Catholics what to do. Then it begins, the only sermon I have ever heard in my entire life that meant anything to me.

He stands next to us, directly in front of the pews. No podium, no notes, and talks to us. He talks of a God who doesn't care if you're Catholic or not, of love transcending man-made division. He talks of loving a child and losing him. He talks of caring enough about your child and his friends to re-experience what must be like another funeral. He talks of pain and sorrow, love and loss.

He talks to Curt, bending down, eye level, reaching out; a private communication. He talks of brothers fighting each other and being annoyed and yet loving each other. He becomes a twelve year-old. He asks questions and Curt answers.

He talks to Michelle about being a teenager, about death, about love and loss. It is as if he has known us all our lives, this total stranger who knows all the right words. It seems as if he talks for 10 minutes. It's been 45.

Then come more prayers and more music. He serves Communion. At the end of the service, he asks those there to introduce themselves to us. They come, telling us who they are and how they knew Lee. Some of Lee's friends, the boys who arranged the service, hug us. We thank them. They have buried their friend in their own way. I get the feeling that they now believe he is safe, having been through their ritual. It is caring and beautiful. I thank the priest for his time and the obvious effort. The service has lasted an hour and a half.

I get a letter later from a friend who is a member of that church. She says that they have never done anything like that before in their church. "Your son must have been very special." Yes, he was, and so are his friends.

June 3rd

We had to go to a wake last night. A friend of Ted's from work died of a coronary. Never sick, 54 years old. The funeral home was 15 miles away. Ted and I both grew up in that town. The strange thing was that it took us over an hour to get there. We got off the road and took the least direct path. I wonder if it was Freudian avoidance. Both of us knew it would be hard. We talked about Lee all the way there.

We knew no one there. The wife remembered our faces, but not where she had met us or our names. I said she had been at our son's funeral. Her eyes filled with tears and she held me and said, "Then you know what sorrow is." We chatted briefly. Ted spoke of the qualities he had respected in her husband. We stood briefly at the casket. Ted commented that it didn't look like Joe, but "Lee looked just like himself." I cried as we walked to the car and realized my ring was digging into my fingers from the pressure. Ted and I had been holding hands the whole time, squeezing strength into each other, unaware.

I thought about the comment, "Then you know what sorrow is," and I'm puzzled because I don't know. I know I am supposed to. After all, isn't it normal to feel sorrow when your child is dead? But what is it? I guess a combination of things, mostly pain, aching, wanting – pain which is, above all, unrelieved. It is there in some form, all day and all night. I can't change it or ease it or ignore it. I see Lee in the emergency room, I see him at home, I see him on TV shows and in the mall. It's not that I actually *see* him, I just get flashes in my mind of a big, blond, clumsy kid laughing. I want him back and I can't have him. I have never felt this helpless or hopeless.

People keep asking me about the anger I must feel. It's odd, but I don't feel anything I can identify as anger. Anger takes more energy than I have. I feel dead. I feel numb, but I am not angry. I feel exhausted, not physically but mentally. It's as if the effort of functioning without emotion absorbs all of me. By night I could sleep standing up, not from physical exertion, but from the effort it takes to appear as normal as I can. The strange thing is that it's getting harder, not easier. So much for the "time heals" theory people keep offering me.

I am afraid I am running out of reserves. It's as though I was an hour glass filled with sand. At the beginning, I was full and then Lee's death opened a hole in me and since then, little by little, my self is running out.

June 4th

Toxicology Reports

The lawyers have asked me the results. The insurance agents have mentioned them. The nurse in the emergency Room asked me if Lee had been drinking. Michelle has been asked at school if the rumors were true that Lee was bombed out of his mind. The first thing anyone thinks when a teenager is in an auto accident is that they were drunk or drugged. I think it. Now I know how it hurts, knowing people out there thought that was the cause.

When the nurse in the ER asked, I had to respond, "I don't know. He was with friends." I knew deep down inside the answer was *no,* but I'm also realistic. I remember being a teen and sneaking a beer. I'm not naive enough to believe that my eighteen year-old wouldn't, even though I'd never seen it.

When the lawyer asked if Lee drank or took drugs, I said, "No," and then said I didn't have any proof. I knew Lee was not on drugs. He was high on life, not chemicals. He felt contempt for people who "*wasted themselves.*"

I called the coroner's office. "The reports take two to six weeks." I wondered if they really do, or if they are hiding something. Paranoia again.

The reports arrived, seven weeks after the funeral. I am not surprised at the results. I am surprised at my reaction. The tests showed no alcohol, no drugs. I wish I could put them in the paper under the heading,

For all of you who thought he was drunk...

I'm sorry, All it means to me is that he was aware and alert and he felt it. I cry again.

June 5th

• •

Another Funeral

Another funeral home visit last night. The father of a friend of Ted's, seventy-five years old, arthritic. Beverly, the daughter-in-law, meets me at the door to the room where the casket stands, hugs me and whispers, "Don't come in here. You don't have to come in here." I hug back and say, "What difference does it make?"

Carol, Ted's cousin, sees that I am shaky and begins asking staccato, rapid-fire questions about my job: How do you like it? What's it like? How many people work for you? Did you get new office furniture? How long does it take you to drive to work? I am momentarily confused. I can't remember any of the answers to her questions. I can't imagine why she's asking. I frantically search my mind for numbers and answers. Her voice seems very loud and yet very far away. At one point, I think I said that it took me 200 people to drive to work and yet she keeps asking. It dawns on me that she is trying to distract me and has instinctively helped me cover and regain control. I am grateful and I hate it, all at the same time. I never realized how very much I dislike needing help, or how important it is to me to be in control of myself in public. I find myself being ushered to a lounge in the basement surrounded by people talking about everything but death. I nod and chat. We say goodbye and leave and tears are running down my face as we walk to the car.

Ted and I haven't eaten so we stop at a little restaurant in Crown Point on our way home. A group of about twenty people I worked with five years ago are in the back room celebrating a retirement. I am spotted, so I stop in to say, "Hello." Many of these people had been at Lee's funeral. I feel like I am back there again. Am I imagining, or are people looking at me differently? Eye contact is longer, smiles are weaker, my hand gets held more, no one wisecracks. I feel awkward. I wish I weren't there. I tell "how I am doing," and smile on the outside. Someone asks where Ted and I have been that we are eating dinner so late. I say, "At a funeral home." Twenty women fall silent and stay that way.

Ted and I finish dinner and go home. Ted goes to bed. I go into the bathroom and vomit. Then I sit in the living room with a cold washrag, wiping my face, willing my guts to lie still. I stare at the lamp on the piano until 3:00 a.m.

Graduation

• •

Graduation is Sunday. Ted and I had decided two or three weeks ago that we would not go. It just seemed to be too difficult to deal with. I called the school with he intention of telling them we would not be there and expressing our thanks for the invitation. Ms. Matsiak, the counselor, began telling me of the plans the seniors had made for a candlelight ceremony. It seems that a group of seniors and the principal, who were in charge of planning the graduation program, had included a memorial service for Lee. I started crying. I felt like an idiot. I hated that I was doing it, but I couldn't help it. I have never in my life cried with strangers and I am appalled at my own lack of control. The counselor doesn't know what to say. I really didn't want to go, and now there is no way I can not go. I feel torn. It seems like a needless beating of my emotions again and yet I must be there for some reason. If I don't go I'll regret it, so I go and I dread it.

June 8th

· ·

The gym is packed. They're all jostling and smiling and jockeying for a better camera position. There's a carnival mood, everyone happy and proud. I feel that I am the only person there who is hurting. I feel isolated and alone in the middle of 3,000 people. There are 437 graduates, all to be seated in chairs on the gym floor. The bleachers are full up to the ceiling, people jammed against each other. The buzz of conversation never seems to stop. It is noisy and not at all solemn. I feel very old. I remember graduations as hushed and important. It seems more like a party. I am sorry I am here. The organist begins to play according to the program. The graduating class begins to march in; boys in purple, girls in white, each carrying a long-stemmed red rose. The spectators wave and signal to the child who is theirs. The kids look as though they wish their parents would behave. Yet I can imagine what the parents are feeling. I am jealous. The speaker begins saying traditional things about challenges and memories and futures. The people around me are talking about how hot it is and how many open houses they are going to.

They are beginning to hand out the diplomas now, calling out scholarships won by each student. There are self-conscious handshakes with the president of the school board, shaky descent off the stage by girls unaccustomed to high heels. Row after row of young people are moving to the stage. It seems like an endless line. My back aches and my legs are shaking. When they reach the place in the alphabet where Lee's name would have been read. I stare straight ahead. They don't say it and I am ready, stainless steel again, for the omission.

The graduates are about half-way through receiving their diplomas. Those who have them are getting restless, squirming in chairs, shuffling their feet. Those waiting are talking to each other. The noise is getting louder. Someone has a whistle, a foghorn-loud irritating noise that gets more and more frequent. Out of nowhere a beach ball appears, floating and bouncing, being tossed about by the gowned graduates, a symbolic defiance of school rules and decorum. I am nauseated. The memorial to Lee is next and I will be sick if this circus prevails. I desperately wish I could leave before I see what I am afraid will be disrespectful, a laughing, silly travesty of a tribute to the young man I mourn. I am wedged in the middle of the row and cannot move or I would run. Gaudily dressed mothers strutting to meet their diploma-clutching daughters are presenting them with bouquets of roses. I am sick with fear that I will see all these people not care about Lee.

It is time.

The tassels have been moved and the class has been pronounced graduates and the crowd has cheered, clapped and whistled. The talking continues. The minister walks to the microphone. Two girls are sitting behind me. One, reading the program, says, "Who's Lee Musser?" The other says, "Remember? He's that guy who got killed in the car wreck. He made a wide turn and"—I turn around and say, "I'm his mother." She says, "I'm sorry." They don't speak again.

The president of the senior class lights a tall pillar candle on the stage. Valedictorian, salutatorian, class officers, all light tall candles from it and light one candle in each row of graduates. The tiny flames are passed down the rows until each senior standing holds a tiny flickering light. The gym lights are turned off and only candles are visible. *And it is totally, utterly, completely still.*

The minister speaks of life flickering out early like a candle flame. He talks of Lee and his competitiveness and musicianship. He says that the graduates need to think of how Lee would have challenged them to succeed and do their best. It remains quiet. Flash bulbs break the darkness, recording a truly beautiful sight. I find I am holding my breath. It is over. It was beautiful, caring and dignified. In my mind I thank them all for remembering.

The noise begins again and it doesn't matter. The graduation is over and again everyone around me is happy. I am alone and lonelier than I have ever been. I go to the front of the gym and the principal hands me Lee's diploma. The only one left on the table. The gym is clearing. I walk slowly to the car, clutching Lee's diploma to my chest. Several people I know meet my eyes. My arm gets squeezed by someone. I think to myself, *Why?* Then stainless steel again.

June 12th

● ●

Freda called. Freda is a thoroughly likeable, somewhat eccentric study in contrasts. She is the Dean of a School of Nursing and a patchwork quilt of traits. Petite and blonde with a china-doll aura of fragility, she can and does defend her position. She has a wry sense of humor and an eleven year-old's giggle. She is educated and intellectual and was an instructor of mine in a graduate nursing course. I respect her intelligence and her down-to-earth insistence that her values are important. We have been professionally touching bases for years, not close friends and yet I feel comfortable with her. I have gotten over some, but not all, of the awe I felt toward her. The teacher-student mentality seems to be a hang-up for me. My own lack of confidence, I guess.

We make plans for dinner and a drink and I wonder why she called.

We sit at a booth in the bar and talk about school and my plans for finishing my master's degree. We talk about my getting a doctorate. It's an idea I find humorous. I do not consider myself intellectual or even intelligent enough to complete the required course work. The discussion turns to self-images as opposed to how others perceive us. It is a contrast that never fails to astound me. I see myself as shy and reserved, basically an average, ordinary person who tries hard to achieve. I think I have fairly good taste but I'm not really extraordinary in anything – kind of a Jill of all trades, master of none.

Freda tells me that if I were ordinary she wouldn't be sitting here. That I am schizoid, reserved at times and off the wall at other times. She says I am "a class act." I'm stunned. When a role model tells you they respect *you,* it's a shock.

We talk of my son. I express the fear that people may think I'm not grieving because I have, I think, been successful at appearing to be normal. Freda looks puzzled and says, "But would anyone have expected anything else? You are a person whom people see as dignified and reserved. Any other behavior would be out of keeping with who you are." I wonder if I know who I am anymore. Maybe I never did.

I find out that Freda's doctorate is in psych and counseling. On the way home I wonder if I have been psyched and counseled. I wonder if the whole point of our meeting was a kind gesture of support, an attempt to build up a faltering person. She meets with my boss. Maybe I have been assessed and found to be needing professional help and I don't even know it. It is a terrifying thought.

June 15th

●●

I haven't talked to my friend Mary for over a week. I haven't called or seen her. It's deliberate. I have begun to feel like a burden. I feel that every time we are together I am a depressing downer, no fun to be with anymore. I sense a reticence on her part, a guarding. She's being careful not to touch on anything that might hurt me, an almost visible emotional cotton batting, wrapping me in protective custody. She doesn't want to say the wrong thing, yet she wants to be helpful and supportive. I feel sorry for her, stuck with a friend who used to be compatibly crazy and now is quietly apathetic. Somehow, when I'm with her I can drop my normal act. I sit and don't react. I talk of pain and fears, expecting and receiving her quiet acceptance. I hadn't thought before now of how hard that must be for her. I stop calling on her for help, wanting to spare her the stress and at the same time testing the strength of her friendship. Maybe she wants out. Maybe she's tired of being a frequently cried upon shoulder. Maybe she doesn't want to continue the strong-man role I've cast her in. Maybe she just doesn't know how to get out. I don't call her and I hope I'm wrong. The phone doesn't ring.

We usually go shopping and have lunch on Saturday. I'm up and dressed at 7:30 a.m. waiting, but the phone doesn't ring. So I guess I'm right. I read an article that said friendships often end after one of the friends bares her soul to the other and comes to regret it.

Maybe I've leaned too hard. Maybe I've overwhelmed her with my needs and have forgotten hers. I feel selfish, punished and alone. I cry and mourn the loss of my friend.

Everybody's searching for a hero.
People need someone to look up to.
Never found anyone who fulfilled my need.
A lonely place to be.
And so I learned to depend on me.

I decided long ago never to walk
in anyone's shadow.
If I fail, I succeed, at least
I lived as I believe.
No matter what they take from me,
they can't take away my dignity.

From: The Greatest Love of All*

June 17th

● ●

Ted went to the cemetery again tonight. He goes two or three times a week and sits alone, staring at Lee's grave. I don't really understand the need to do it. I've been there twice. I find no solace in staring at a grave, no comfort in a cemetery. Lee is not there. I want to remember his life and his aliveness, not his death.

It upsets Ted to go. He cries and even the crying upsets him. I try to understand. I don't know how to approach it or even if I should. I ask him if it makes him feel better. "No, it makes me feel worse." "Then why do you go there?"

"I don't know. It's on my way home from work. I just end up there." Shrugging of shoulders, tears rolling; a man who never cries, crying. "Why do you go alone?"
"I went alone when Skippy died."
Pause.
"But you were alone then, Ted."
"I love you, Linda-Gal."
"I love you, too. Ted."
We cry.

24

June 19th

Two months today. I'm at work at the hospital and suddenly my eyes fill and spill over. I passed a terrible accident on my way to work today—two semi's. They were pulling a man out of one of the trucks as I passed. It seems that I've seen more traffic accidents in the past two months than I've ever seen in my life. I wonder if I was that unaware or if it is similar to when I was pregnant. I had never noticed how many other women I saw who had a tent dress and an enormous belly. Heightened awareness, I guess. I am never without something that reminds me of Lee or the loss of him. I can somehow "gear up" if I know something is going to be painful and guard against feeling it, but it's the little things that catch you unaware that really hurt. Memory triggers that suddenly project a picture in your mind's eye: a little boy with a balloon, the swimming pool, a song on the radio.

June 20th

I bumped into Mrs. Smith in the hall on the way to my office. I asked what she was doing at the hospital. "Dave and Todd were in a car accident."

Dave has spent weekends at our house. He was a friend of Lee's and played French horn in the band. He's thin, freckled—a fun kid. I don't know the other boy. I ask how they are. Dave has lacerations of the face and is in another local hospital. Todd, this stranger to me, is in Intensive Care here.

I tell myself to stay away, not to go and see him. After all, I don't know him. Lee didn't know him. There is no reason. I would be an intrusion.

Somehow I am there, walking into ICU, glancing at cubicle doors where old bodies lie tethered to bottles and beeping pumps. I see him, head bandaged, unresponsive. He lies flat on his back, barechested with the smooth shoulder of a young boy, not baby fat, yet not defined. I do not enter the cubicle. I sense a person in a corner.

My legs are shaking as I stand in the doorway. The head nurse tells me it's a miracle he's still alive. My palms are sweating and my fingernails are digging into my hand. I know better than to stand there any longer. I walk slowly back to my office and close the door. My chin is quivering and I am fighting, eyes stinging and open wide. I will *not* cry at work!

Heather from Cardiology saw me in ICU. I walk to her office. She takes one look at me and shoos out a tech who looks puzzled and somewhat confused.

"I saw you come out and I knew, Linda. Why don't you go home? You don't need to be here. I pray for you every night. Why don't you let yourself go? You aren't being fair to yourself."

I fight again for control and wonder why I am standing in her office. I refuse to go home. I say I will be alright, and though gritted teeth, "I won't go home because *I don't want to feel it*." I walk out of her office without saying goodbye. I'm sure she must think I'm crazy. *I'm* sure I'm crazy.

I go home and sit and talk with Ted about selling the house. Suddenly I am crying about watching codes and seeing stretchers, hearing ambulances and talking about patients and death and life. All the things that are a routine part of being a nurse and working in the hospital. I lie on my bed and try to think and calm myself down.

I wake up at 8:00 a.m. in my slip, blouse and pantyhose. I don't remember getting undressed at all. I don't think I did. I wonder how much longer I can hang on pretending to be normal.

I go to the kitchen and Ted hands me a cup of coffee and asks, "Are you OK?" I look at him and nod as tears roll down my cheeks. It dawns on me that I am jealous of that shadowy figure in the corner of an ICU cubical. I am jealous and hate her because even with a flat EEG her son is alive. She can still talk to him and hug him and pat his arm and love him. I drink my coffee, wipe my face and do the laundry.

June 21st

The whole issue of death is one I have difficulty coming to any comfortable terms with. I am unable to resolve any feelings or come to acceptance or rationalize any death – not only Lee's. I think the fact is undeniable yet unacceptable. I cannot believe that there is a purpose or design to it. I cannot utilize a belief in a God who "takes people home." I don't know what possible reason there is, and I am not good at taking things on faith.

June 23rd

This business of loss, grief and adjustment is very strange. It teaches you a lot about yourself and about others. There are times I remember when I thought I knew myself pretty well and could predict, pretty much, how I would behave in a given situation. I have never been a person who lets the entire world see the real me. I don't trust enough for that. I am finding it very difficult to keep things inside as well as I once did.

I have always prided myself on being in control, being able to take things in stride and look logically at the options. I'm stymied now because there aren't any options that change the fact of Lee's death. My only choices exist in deciding how to deal with it. I can logically decide what I'm going to do, but since I'm dealing with emotion, it doesn't always work.

I want to be in control of myself, yet sometimes what I really want is to let someone hold me while I sob. I'd like to lie down and let someone rub my back and stroke my hair while I tell them how much I hurt. I want someone to take care of me as though I were a little girl again.

June 26th

• •

Went out with Mary last night. We ate dinner, had a drink and didn't talk about much. Mary seems tired and discouraged. I got the impression she really just wanted to go to bed. I felt sorry that I had bothered her. I am so paranoid lately about being a bother to people.

We left the restaurant and I felt let down. I had not given her any-thing and I felt uncomfortable. We are two people who sincerely care about each other, yet I feel I'm killing our friendship. It's not the same and I don't know if it's because I'm not the same.

In the parking lot Mary hesitates. "Come sit in my car for a minute."

She asks me what's wrong and I don't know what to say. She says I am " looking at her" and I tell her I am concerned and scared that our friendship is failing because of my being such an emotional drain on her.

"I'm playing a role, Mary, it's all a front. I'm not who I used to be but I don't know who I am anymore." "What do you mean? *Talk* to me!" "I can't, Mary. It hurts too much. I'm keeping it inside and I know it, but I can't do anything about it. If I let it out, I'll lose everything emo-tionally." "No you won't, Linda. You're strong. You're stronger than you think you are, and if you go on playing this role you'll be a shell. *(I already am!)* You won't be able to give your two remaining living children what they need and you won't be the person you are capa-ble of being and *I will never forgive you!*"

I try to explain my confusion but I can't seem to make sense of it. I want so much to be able to make someone understand. I am des-perately afraid of revealing my pain to anyone. I talk on and on about pretending to be fine—behaving normally, dressing appropri-ately, not having people pity me.

There is a difference in Mary's comments and questions. She is firmer, voice stronger, accepting no evasions, allowing no cop-outs.

"Why don't you talk about Lee? I haven't heard you mention him for weeks." "I talk about him."

"No, you don't! Only in reference to things – Lee's room, Lee's graduation. You don't talk about him. Tell me about Lee." "I can't." Tears starting to fall. "Tell me about your son, Lee. He was a good son," forcefully. "Don't, Mary," begging "I can't take it."

She stops and I instantly regret it. As hard as it seems, I am sorry I stopped. I can't start again. We sit in silence. Mary says, "You're going to talk to me. You're going to start the grieving and mourning you need to do."

"I can't." "Yes, you can and you will. I have let you lead. I have avoided when you avoided. I have backed off. My questions were tough and they hurt you. I didn't know whether to stop or not. My guts said, *Go* and my emotions said, *Stop*. You've got to talk and get it out and get it over or two years or five years from now, when it hits, it won't be normal."

"There is no time and no place. There are always people around. I know I'm making excuses. I'm angry at myself. I hate people who don't face facts. I despise cowards and I am one."

"There is a place where it is OK to cry in public and there aren't a lot of people around–the cemetery."

She has given me a password, a code we will both understand. All I have to do is tell her I'd like to go there and she will be with me and I am grateful. I wonder if I will ever use it. I mentioned trust to Mary before. I said I didn't trust anyone, including myself. I regret it because I trust her completely. I love her and I don't want to become a burden to her. I can't explain our kinship. We are opposites in many ways, yet there is an underlying closeness. I am very lucky to have her. Please don't let me lose her. I am so damn vulnerable right now.

June 30th

I 've cried more over the last three days than since Lee died. I've said all along that it was my job to support everyone else and that I would someday let it out for me. Maybe I am finally beginning to feel or let myself admit out loud what I am feeling. I don't know why I am fighting so hard not to show the hurt. I've been afraid of it, that it would be so overwhelming I wouldn't be able to function. I was afraid that I would no longer be the person I have worked so hard to become.

I was a shy, scared kid, who sometimes still feels that if anyone saw what was underneath the wisecracking, confident facade, I'd never be able to pull it off. I'm not sure what I'm afraid of—rejection, I guess. There are any number of memories—cruelties to the fattest girl in the sixth grade *(measured by the school nurse),* the kid who skipped half of third grade and earned herself the title of "lard-brain," the girl whose best friend told her she'd hang around only when no boys were watching because she would never get a date if they were seen together.

My style is aloof and reserved, deliberate and professional, and yet I long for the release of a storm of tears and a total expression of the feelings I keep fighting to deny. I know the need is there, yet private tears are excruciatingly lonely. I just can't seem to let myself go in front of anyone else.

Mary called last night and we went to the cemetery. We sat for a while, Lee's grave 20 feet across the road, quiet tears sliding down my cheeks. I said, "I want my kid back. It's not fair. There's no reason." Mary told me I couldn't have my kid back and no, it's not fair, and I probably would never find a reason. Somehow it helped.

July 11th

T he fourth of July has come and gone. We didn't go to the parade. I just didn't want to see the high school band with only one tuba. Every other year there has been a picnic at our house with the whole family going to see Lee march in the parade. This year, nobody was at our house. We went to Mary's for a picnic. It was abominably hot. All I wanted to do was go home and float in the pool. We stayed and watched fireworks, ate, drank, and talked to all the people there.

Mary noticed me losing it. The TV was on, and over the news came the story of some idiot stunt man who locked himself in a box and had a truck hit it at 45 mph for a "thrill show." For some reason it got me. I left the room on the pretense of getting a drink. She followed, hugged me briefly and asked if I was OK. I tried to figure out why I was upset by a stupid newscast. I guess it was the poor effort to defy death, a cheap, tacky stunt that could have killed someone for no good reason. I wonder if there is a good reason. I seem to be searching for a logical explanation to justify in my mind why Lee died. The saddest part of all is that there is none. It is a total, utter waste of a worthwhile person. I guess the *"Why?!"* is starting for me. I find myself thinking about it and force it out of my mind. I'm acting again, playing "Linda Normal."

I haven't been writing. I haven't been feeling it or dealing with it. I get up, go to work, go home, go to bed. I have found myself being animated and enthusiastic about things at work and calmly watching myself perform. I should have been an actress. I even asked my boss for more to do. Maybe it'll help get rid of the inner apathy I feel about everything. I really don't care about much anymore. I do my job, but the challenge and excitement are gone. I just need a paycheck.

I sleep, eat, work, talk, act and react. The only change is that I don't care, and I used to care passionately about things. I read all the articles on how to juggle family and career. I tried to do it all right. I worked for lofty, idealistic motives: nursing, geriatrics, professionalism. I've been a Scout leader and baked school fair cakes. I've been a youth leader at church. I've tried to give my kids a role model to be proud of. I've not deliberately hurt anyone or committed any grievous offenses. I'm learning that I had a very naive philosophy: work hard and rewards will be yours. My reward? Seeing my son dead and bleeding.

July 15th

he kids and Ted are in Wisconsin for three days. To be truthful, I was looking forward to some time alone. I need to be by myself and get in touch with my feelings. I thought that if I were alone, maybe I could release some of the tears and hurt that I've bottled up inside. The odd thing is that even when alone, I play the same role – tough, strong, don't let go. It's ridiculous to not be able to let yourself see you cry, but I kept fighting it until last night.

Mary and I made plans to go out after work. I had to stop at the funeral home. A co-worker's husband died and I felt I should stop. I had geared up. I knew it was going to be hard. It was the same funeral home and I was ready for flashbacks. I also knew I would handle it. I talked with Peg and handled the sense of familiarity. I thought I was doing fine until the funeral director said, "I've got something for you, Linda." He handed me a 12x15 picture frame and I looked down to see Lee looking up at me from the center of a beautiful watercolor poem done in calligraphy. It's the first time I've looked at a picture of Lee since he died. It felt like someone punched me in the stomach. A couple of tears, a quick thank you and I literally ran out of the funeral home.

Mary was picking me up, so I tried, and I mean really tried to pull it together. I thought I did pretty well. We talked of diets and jobs and weather and other insignificant things. Then she drove me home.

I went to get us a drink. Mary sat on the couch, looked at the time and calmly said, "OK, Musser. Talk to me." Just as calmly I talked about surface things, nothing deep or emotional. I was not even near crying. I talked about apathy. I never once looked her in the eye. I focused on a plant, the cat, I said, "I need so badly to let it out, but I can't."

Mary said, "Why not?"

"I don't know – self image, I guess. I can't stand letting anyone see me falling apart. It makes me vulnerable and gives them a way to hurt me."

Suddenly, Mary reached over, grabbed my chin and turned my head toward her. "Don't you know you can let it out with me? Quit fighting it!" All of a sudden there was a release. I was sobbing, crying, being held like a child. Not polite little tears sliding down cheeks, but waves of tearing hurt, grasping for air, noises like an animal in pain.

Choking, crying, I said, "He was just a baby, only 18. I tried so hard to do it right. I took him to the doctor. I taught him to be Somebody. Other kids get in wrecks and aren't killed. Why Lee? Why me? He was just a baby. He never got to do anything. I want him back!" Over and over. "He was just a baby." Mary held me while I sobbed and choked, my stomach heaving, spasms, escalating sobs, begging someone to tell me *why,* pleading to have him back, promising to do anything if only I could have him back.

There was nothing left of the Linda Musser people know, there was only a hurting, crying, out-of-control woman being held like a child. Sobs subsiding, breath still catching, hiccuping, choking, I sit up and pull away. I can't look at Mary's face. Her shoulder and front of her dress are wet and smeared with mascara. Her eyes are watery and she keeps one hand on my arm. I wipe my face and sit sniffling and try to figure out how I can face her and not feel like a fool or a weakling. I am embarrassed, so I say, "So much for image," bitter sounding, even to me. Mary says, "Bullshit." I try to give what is supposed to be a laugh. It comes out a snorting noise. We sit quietly, not saying anything.

It is late. I feel guilty that Mary's family is wondering where she is or worried about her. She gets up to leave and reaches around to hug me. I start to pull away and suddenly I hug back. Two grown women hugging. She's holding me up and I'm hanging on for dear life. I whisper, "Don't be too nice to me or I'll start again." She says she doesn't want to leave me like this. I shrug and say, "Don't worry – I'm tough," and I give that snorting, bitter laugh again. She walks to her car and I walk back into the house and lock the door. I can feel my eyelids swelling already. I know I'll look like hell in the morning. I take a bath, lie in bed and try not to think. I sleep.

It's morning. I look like hell.

July 22nd

There is no way to explain what it feels like. People keep asking me how I feel. There are times when I feel it's none of their business. I think some are curious. I think others ask to be polite. I sense they want to hear, "just fine." Then they can make the appropriate response, "if you ever need to talk, call me", pat my arm and walk away relieved.

Others never ask. I think some of them can't deal with it themselves. They're the ones whose eyes slide to the baseboard when conversations move to dangerous ground. I sometimes feel like I have leprosy. I resent the fact that I seem to spend more time making them feel comfortable than vice versa.

Once I tried being honest. I said, "What do you want, the stock answer or the truth?" I realized it didn't give him much choice, but I didn't care. He mumbled, "The truth," and I said, "I'm bleeding to death emotionally but I keep going." He never asked again.

Every now and then I get the feeling that somebody really wants to know, so I open up a little and give a taste of what I'm feeling. I frequently find that what they really wanted was a chance to talk about their grief. It's interesting. I end up comforting someone else. It leaves me feeling tired and angry and used.

There are people out there who could help me, but I seem to send messages that I don't want to talk. I guess I just come across as unapproachable. I refuse to allow myself to fall apart at work or in front of my kids or in public or if it makes others feel worse. It doesn't leave a lot of options, but it's the only cope I've got. My self esteem would not handle well a picture of me blubbering in the cafeteria.

It's incredible the dumb things I worry about. When nothing is really important to you, little things become very important. I seem to care more about details. Maybe it's because I have concluded that the little things are the only things I can control. The big things just happen by themselves.

July 25th

I guess I'm changing. It may be that I have changed or it may be that my perception has changed. I feel more sure of myself. It may be thanks to my new job. I've been at it about six months. My evaluation was positive. Considering that it's a job I was afraid to go after, that's pretty heady stuff in itself.

I think the other part has to do with Lee's death. When the worst possible thing in the world has happened to you, nothing else seems all that intimidating. I've been hurt so badly that nothing seems scary. I've survived the worst loss there is, so what more frightening thing can there be?

Mary says she sees a change. I press for details and words like, "arrogant, cocky, ruthless and manipulative" are suddenly lying between us in glowing capital letters. I laugh a lot, but it scares me. Am I all that she says? I'm not sure I want to be that. We talk about differences: "Some people have goals and others accept the status quo." Out of the blue I say, "Some people kill themselves." There is a long silence. I have no idea why I said it, what it means, or if it means anything. Strange. I wonder if Mary…

I stopped writing this and left to do something. I returned and have absolutely no idea what I was going to write. It's all jumbled gob-bledygook in my head. Thoughts are like smoke floating in and out, not connecting with anything or with each other. I feel very disconnected.

August 1st

I finally did it. I cleaned out Lee's closet and sorted his things. I don't know why I hadn't done it before. I just didn't do it.

It was a gorgeous Saturday; one of those days with marshmallow clouds and a shocking blue sky, a day that screamed for everyone to be outside. I am inside cleaning closets. I started with mine, ruthlessly throwing out clothes, tacky shoes, purses with broken straps.

I sorted through blouses and too-tight skirts. I rigidly arranged blouses together, skirts together, shoes all pointing in the same direction.

Next came Curt's closet. He's an 11 year-old sports nut who saves sweats with torn off sleeves as though they were a national treasures. I find a fishing rod slipped through the sleeve of his only suit. Stuck in the corner on the floor are the mates to socks long gone.

I attacked Ted's closet with a vengeance. It's easy to get rid of things that aren't yours. By the time I finish there are three giant plastic garbage bags full, ready to go. Job well done! Closets are clean.

I find myself at the linen closet sorting through old prescriptions and faded pillowcases. I'm tired but unsatisfied. Suddenly I realize that all of this has been the preparation. It's normal to clean closets. I go to Lee's room and begin to sift through the remainders and reminders.

I turn on the stereo. It's hard rock with a driving beat. I pull things from his closet. There is a stack of T-shirts, jeans, his good black shoes, dress slacks he wore to a job interview. I wonder where his navy blue sport coat is, and it dawns on me that he was buried in it. I am crying and yet not crying. I am a house cleaning robot with tears falling down my face. I stack clothes neatly, t-shirts in one pile — Michelle and Curt may want them — sweaters too large for anyone else go in a box. I find a sweater I bought him for Christmas still in the Christmas box. He must not have liked it.

I package, pack, stack and bundle. I stand back and realize how very little there is. I neatly replace everything in his closet. What do I do with it? I can't throw out binoculars, cameras and computers. Everyone else's closet is full. The only sensible thing is to leave it in the only empty closet in the house. So I have accomplished what? Most of the same things go back in the same closet, only now there are no clothes hanging there. I take my winter clothes, some in dry cleaner bags, and neatly arrange them in a row. It is still Lee's closet. It is still Lee's things. I'm exhausted and deep inside I know I haven't done anything, really. It is still Lee's room.

I know he's not coming home again. I know I should move everything out and re-do the room. But what's the harm? Maybe someday I'll be ready. But not now. So be it.

One thing seems strange and painful in a dull kind of way. Such an active, vital young man didn't leave anything important. I don't know what I mean, really, it's just that when you sort all the things out, they're just objects. But each one has a memory tied to it. I'm afraid that if I toss out the things, the memories will go, too. God, it hurts to remember, but it hurts a thousand times more to think that anyone could forget.

August 14th

I find myself more confident in some situations. At work, I think I project a confident, capable image. People are starting to turn to me for advice. I'm more willing to speak my mind and take risks. I am less hesitant and more forceful. In the back of my mind, I keep saying, "It makes no difference. Nothing worse can happen to me." I will be finishing my Master's and I really think I've become more of who I always wanted to be in my job.

On the other hand, my personal relationships are deteriorating. I'm irritable with family and withdrawn from friends. I'm impatient with my mother. I haven't really talked to her about Lee, and I don't understand it. I've always been very close to her and yet I have almost withdrawn completely.

I get immediately angry with Ted's parents for no reason. I basically avoid them even when they're here. I haven't begun to explore why.

Mary says I'm withdrawing from her. We have little or no contact. No more long involved discussions, very surface, very old acquaintance, very guarded. I hadn't realized it, but she's right.

I try to explain that I want or maybe need sometimes to be led and not be the leader. I think she feels I have to set the pace of our relationship at this point. She's still protecting me. I can't seem to get across to anyone that right now I want someone to tell me what I am doing and take charge of me. Nobody understands that I don't have the energy or the courage to ask for help. Nobody believes me when I say I'm not facing it or that I'm not coping. The facade works too damn well. Even the people who know me best are believing it and I need desperately for one of them to cut through the act and let me cry again. Mary's done it a couple of times, but I can't stomach the idea that our relationship is based on me crying every time we're together. I'm just tired of being strong. Who's there for me? A lot of the time the answer is no one. It's incredibly lonely and I'm feeling sorry for myself again.

August 17th

● ●

Mary and I are driving to the fairgrounds to meet our husbands and children. We're going to see a horse show at the county fair. Beautiful sunny day with a nice August evening. We're comfortable not saying much. Suddenly, a car pulls out in front of us. Mary slams on the brakes, honks the horn and I see the back of a car coming too close and too fast. All at once I am in Lee's car with him at the time of the accident. I see headlights, hear horns and tires screaming. I know I am going to hit. I am in terror. I feel pain. I hear breaking glass and crumpling metal. I feel myself hit the steering wheel. I hear a scream and a moan. I realize it's me and I'm shaking all over. Mary touches my arm and says, "Are you all right?" I nod, "Yes," even though I am still shaking. We ride in silence for a few blocks. I can see Mary glancing at me as she drives. The other car has turned down a side street and is gone. I say, "I wonder if Lee had time to honk the horn." Mary says, "I'm sorry." I try to tell her it's not her fault. She just shakes her head. I'm still shaking.

Every night now I see headlights coming toward me when I lie down to sleep.

Phases I Have Learned to Hate

• •

How are you doing?
What am I supposed to be doing? Nothing can be done.

You are doing so well.
How would you know? True, I'm not embarrassing you. I'm being a good girl. I'm not screaming or sitting in a corner sucking my thumb. It doesn't mean I don't want to, and I still might.

I feel so sorry for you.
Welcome to the club. I feel sorry for me, too.

Take it day by day.
Take what? Pain? A day is like eternity. Hour by hour might work. Some hours are forever.

Time heals.
Time passes. Passes over the hole in your existence. Time covers the wound with scar tissue, with ragged edges.

God will comfort you.
If there is a God, I think he's vicious and cruel. I don't go for a God who kills innocents.

You need to let it out. Go ahead and cry.
On command? At your convenience? In a grocery store? In front of my 90 year-old grandmother who feels guilty for living?

I admire you. If it were me, I don't know what I'd do.
I don't know what I'd do either. I still don't know, but I'm doing. One doesn't plan it, one just does.

Have you thought about professional help?
I've spent my life as a nurse, being there for others. Now I need to pay someone to talk to them? Do you think I'm crazy?

Additional Hurts

Buying too many bananas. Less laundry.
The day the sympathy cards stopped coming.
Reading the autopsy report."This is the body of a young white male"
Finding a pair of dirty socks under his bed.
Being asked how many children I have. I can't say, "two," yet.

August 25th

I am weak, tired, tearful, struggling. I am so close to tears so much of the time that my eyes feel like sand boxes. I haven't worn my contact lenses for fear of damage to my swollen eyes. I cry and ache inside. The pain seems bigger lately, or maybe the pain isn't bigger, my resistance is just smaller.

I vacillate between wanting to dissolve in tears and wanting to never feel another emotion again. I am wounded by my failure to hide it, my pride in the dirt, dignity, like broken china, in pieces on the floor. I have been seen at my worst or weakest – or is it most wounded?

Labor Day

I don't know what it is that I want. I shift between a total inability to talk about my feelings and a driving need to spill my guts that is almost physical. I don't understand my feelings. I went to Mary's yesterday knowing I needed to talk, yet when I got there I didn't say anything. I ended up cleaning a closet of hers! I have no idea why or how that even got started. All I know is that suddenly I was rearranging things that didn't belong to me and telling the person who owned them that she should throw some of them out. Later, we sat on the sofa and ignored a baseball game on TV. Suddenly, I couldn't stand it and said I had to go. I cried most of the way home, leaking sad tears.

September 2nd

I think I need professional help! I'm having a lot of trouble controlling my emotions. I'm having trouble identifying my feelings. I'm depressed, tearful and sad. At other times I'm confused. I have not admitted to feeling anger. I'm not sure if that's because I'm denying having it or denying feeling it. I don't feel angry, only mortally wounded. I'm frustrated at my inability to reach Michelle. She's hurting and struggling with her feelings, but she won't let me in. I'm so proud of her and I want to help her, but I can't penetrate the barrier. I feel I'm failing as a mother. I try to respect her need to maintain her cool. What a rotten example I must be setting for her. I guess I've taught her to build a shell around herself. Maybe it's her cope, yet I think she needs to talk. I've tried to get her to talk to Mary. She hasn't. I want her to talk to someone, but I really want it to be me. This is humbling in a lot of ways.

I've given up on pride and dignity. I fell apart in front of Mary and Larry the other day. Mike came over to the house to say goodbye before he left for Purdue. We talked briefly. I wished him good luck and all the usual stuff one says to an 18 year-old on his own for the first time. He reached out and hugged me. At that moment, it was Lee I was hugging and I ached with pain. Why isn't this my son? Mike left and I sat for a few minutes and tried to get hold of myself. Larry and Ted were at the table talking and I sat down and started to cry. I kept apologizing for crying. Larry leaned over and talked about a time he had cried and how it was all right to cry and how he and Mary wanted to help. There was something different about him. I knew he was revealing a part of himself that few people see. I knew it was costing him something to share his own hidden pain. I felt it was a moment that was the epitome of caring and I know it won't happen again. I will cherish the memory and wonder again and again what I have done to earn such good friends.

Another issue is raising its head. I made a remark the other day about faith and my rejection of religion. Mary looked at me and said something about how she felt I was desperately seeking it. I suppose one of these days I'll have to look at my feelings about religion. I'm not ready for that yet.

September 4th

• •

Michelle brought her new high school yearbook home. Things have certainly changed since I was in school! This was a glossy, slick, professional-looking book with color pictures and sophisticated lay-outs.

There is a black-bordered box with Lee's name and date of birth. The date of his death is wrong. There is a picture of the candlelight ceremony at graduation. The Lee Musser Memorial Award is listed with the name of the first winner.

This thing that got to me was a picture of Lee giving a speech. It's a candid shot, unposed. It captures his intensity when he was concentrating. I can see his tension. I remember him practicing that speech, pacing frantically across the living room. He was terrified of public speaking. He joked nervously about needing all the points he could get, so he wore a suit and tie, bucking peer wisecracks, going for the grade. It's the suit he was buried in. He loved to argue a point and spent hours conning his Dad and me into discussions of our philosophical differences: Ted the conservative versus Lee the liberal. They both loved it.

I miss his energy and his presence. God, how I miss him!

September 23rd

● ●

I called Mary, thinking I might cheer her up or at least support her through a hard time at work and suddenly tears are falling and I ask, "When does it start to stop hurting? I am tired of it. I am worn out and exhausted. I am fed up with the wearing down of my defenses and the constant battles with myself to build me back up. I don't want to deal with it anymore. I'm tired and I want a vacation from my feelings." Then I say, "OK, you win."

Mary asks me who I'm talking to. "The big bad guy in the sky who's out to get me."

I have been fighting to retain some semblance of me. I feel now that it's not worth the effort. It's not getting easier or more copeable. It's a constant, wearing pressure. My shell is being worn down and eventually it will crumble and I will turn to white powdery dust, trickling down into nothing.

Every day there is some little reminder. Some days there are big reminders. Curt was lying on the sofa the other night. I glanced over and out of the corner of my eye, I saw Lee in the casket. They look so much alike, it hurts. I walk down the hall at work and there is a young man coming towards me. He doesn't look like Lee at all, and yet there is something about his jaw line that reminds me of Lee. For that instant, it's as though someone stabbed me and the hurt is intense and breathtaking. I have become an expert at tilting my head a certain way and opening my eyes wider so the tears won't fall down my face.

September 30th

● ●

I find myself being very possessive of the things that belong to him. *(I just noticed that I used the present tense. I meant to say, belonged to him. Freudian.)* I want to keep them and I can't imagine what for. I say "maybe Curt will want them," yet I knew they'll be out of style before he grows into them. I just can't bear to throw them out. I feel slightly pathological about it. I should do it and get it over with, but I don't. Maybe I'm pretending he's coming back. I don't want a gravestone. I won't go order one. A gravestone is a visible symbol of reality.

I could turn his room into an office, but it's Lee's room. The bed's still made. There are a couple of his shirts lying there. I keep saying I'll do it when I'm ready, but I'm not getting any readier.

October 21st

● ●

The Weekend

I have just experienced the most incredible weekend of my life! I am so involved in trying to sort out my feelings or at least identify what happened that I can't concentrate on anything else.

Mary and I went to a cottage in Plymouth for the weekend. We had no particular schedule or any particular mad rush of things to do. I think we both wanted some time away to sort through things. I expected some heavy analytical discussion. We have a tendency to do that. What I did not expect was the change I feel inside. I really have some kind of emotional hangover.

We arrived at the cottage Friday evening. It's a gray-stained cedar, A-Frame on a small lake, rustic but not primitive. We roughed it with indoor plumbing and nice wine. We drove around for awhile, looking for a place to eat, talking about day-to-day things. Mary built a fire in the fireplace and we sat sipping wine and watching flames flickering. It would have been Lee's nineteenth birthday. I had a sense of deadness inside me. I didn't mention him at all. Quietly, Mary said, *"Do you want to talk, Linda?"* I shrugged my shoulders and replied, *"I don't think so. You've heard it all before anyway."* Then I started to talk.

I talked about Lee, about my feelings, about things in general. Tears were sliding down my face. I sobbed. I remember talking for a long time about how alone I felt. I spoke of anger toward my family, childhood hurts and years-ago problems. I talked about feelings about God and my hatred toward people who believe. If God watches every sparrow, I cried, it would have been nice if he'd have quit birdwatching and taken care of my son.

I remember crying and asking, *Why!* Mary sat quietly, watching me, occasionally asking a question, gently probing, waiting. I remember admitting that I was pretending Lee was away at school. I remember saying I was a rotten person. I talked for six hours. I cried, became exhausted, relived a lot of my life. It was like watching a movie in my mind.

Mary was sympathetic and accepting. If I sobbed she hugged me and stroked my hair. I felt comforted as I used to when I was a little girl. She mothered me and let me know it was OK. I went to bed feeling drained and empty and exhausted. She was still up staring at the fire when I lay down.

I woke up early Saturday. Mary had been up for a long time. We got dressed and went into town and wandered around a few stores, picked up lunch and went back to the cabin and ate. I wondered while we ate what Mary's reason was for coming here. Finally, she went out on the deck overlooking the lake and said, *"Come out and talk to me."* I didn't. Instead, I started to cry again.

I sat on the porch and cried. I went into the living room and cried. I stood in the bathroom and cried. I went into my bedroom and put a pillow over my face and cried. I didn't want her to hear me, yet I did. I kept waiting for her to come inside. When she did, she lay down on the sofa and slept. I don't remember when she woke or how we started talking again. I remember sitting on the end of the sofa with tears rolling again. She was standing.

"How many children do you have?" She asked.
"Do you want the first answer that comes to my head."
"I want the truth!"
"Three. Two."
"Tell me about your children."
"You know my children." (Stubborn resistance.)
"Tell me about your children." (Hard voice, even, controlled.)
"Curtis is eleven, hates school, loves football. Michelle is sixteen, gorgeous, sensitive, dramatic. Lee is eighteen, 6'1, logical, funny."
I'm crying again, fists balled in my eyes.
"How old is Lee?"
"He was nineteen yesterday!" (Sobbing, pleading.)
"What did you get him for his birthday?" She is pacing up and down, never looking at me, sarcastic.
I am sobbing, not answering her.
Mary is standing, gazing out the window. "At that age, he's probably at school. Where is he?"
I don't answer, I just sit hunched into a ball, wiping my face with a wet washcloth she had handed me. "Where is he, Purdue?"
"Yes." (Whispered lie.)
"I'll bet you talk to him on the phone a lot." (Such a deadly, quiet voice. She's standing, holding the back of a chair.)
"He doesn't have one."
"I'll bet you get lots of letters from him."
"Kids at school don't write letters."
"They do for money." (Bitter-sounding.)
"He has money. He worked all summer to get it."
"When is he coming home?" (Challenging, daring. I feel afraid.)
I say nothing.
"You're a liar! Where is he?!"
"He was killed in a car accident when he was eighteen!" (Torn out of me.)
"How are you doing?" (Eyes averted, tough.)
"Just fine!" (Defiant, loud, angry.)
"How are you doing?" (Insistent, demanding.)
"Just fine!" (Desperate, begging, wanting so badly to believe it.)

Suddenly, she walks away, outside, leaving me alone. I see her slowly walking, head down, staring at the water. I have never felt so lonely or abandoned in my life. I'm afraid. I'm guilty for what I am doing to her. I want to go to her and tell her I'm sorry. I'm afraid I have ended a friendship that means so much to me. I sit and wait, terrified and alone, overwhelmed by guilt.

She slowly returns and sits quietly staring at the water. After what seems like forever, I find a voice and ask, *"Why did you leave?"*

"You said you were doing just fine, and since this is an honest relationship, I know you would not lie to me, so there was nothing else to say. I went out to get some fresh air."

"I'm not fine and we both know it." (Small voice, quiet admission, surrender.)

"Then you've got to admit that Lee is dead and he's not coming back and start to deal with it."

I feel whipped and trampled. I'm exhausted.

"Go wash your face and let's go get supper. When we get back we'll talk about being honest with yourself." She's not questioning. She's saying what will be. I go wash my face. I am compliant. I'm beaten, drained. I have given up.

We go to a little tavern about eight miles away. Mary reminisces about the small town where she grew up. I feel disconnected. We both sit in silence.

Back at the cottage, Mary builds another fire and we sit staring into the flames. I begin to talk again. I am calmer, quieter, only talking and staring into the fire. I hear Mary talking about professional counseling, psychologists, support groups. I notice I am beginning to tremble.

I tell Mary I will not go to a support group and listen to other people re-live their grief. I will not be a part of a bunch of amateur psychologists offering support to each other. I tell her I can't afford the fees charged by shrinks and I won't go to a stranger for help. In a

flat, very firm voice, Mary says, "You can't afford not to go."
I'm not trembling anymore. I'm shaking violently. A great chill has come over me. I can't control it or stop it. I am clutching myself, trying to wrap my own arms tightly around me to hold myself steady. Mary doesn't move or come near me. I make some remark about never having seizures before. My stomach is rolling, teeth chattering. I say, "What's wrong with me?" Mary says, in that same, flat, hard voice, "You're scared shitless," and I know she's right. I listen to her tell me I am afraid of facing the truth. I listen to her tell me that I have to believe and accept the fact that Lee is dead and not coming back. I listen to her tell me that I have been running away from it like a scared little girl. I listen to her tell me I have got to accept the pain and hurt and anger and learn to live in spite of it. I listen to her tell me I am not dealing with it and that until I do, I will never progress past it. I am still shaking when I go to bed. When she turns the light out in her room across the hall, I call softly, *"Mary?"*
"Yeah?"
"Love ya, Gilbert." I say it because it is true. I know how much she's tried to help me. I feel I've failed.
"Same here, Musser."
I fall asleep immediately, exhausted and dead inside.

I wake up at 4:30 a.m. Mary is still sleeping. I move silently to the living room, make coffee and sit on the sofa. I am calm and rational. I am engrossed in thinking through the jumble in my head. At some point, several hours later, I know where I am and where I've got to be. I also know where I have just been. There is no way I can describe the process I went through in my mind. It just seemed to happen. Suddenly, the pieces seemed to fall into place, things began making sense. I hear Mary get up and I tell her the coffee's made. She sits with her coffee and says, "What are you doing up so early?" I reply, *"I've been sitting and thinking and making decisions."*

She is quiet, watching me silently. I swallow hard and look at her and shake my head. There is a lump in my chest the size of a basketball. I look her directly in the eye and say slowly – but the words do get out – *"Lee is dead and he's never coming back. There is nothing I can do to change it."* Tears are sliding down my cheeks, but I have said it and believed it for the first time. "It's a first step," Mary whispers.

I am weeping quiet tears. I whisper, *"I have two children. My oldest son was killed in a car wreck when he was eighteen. He was a terrific kid and I miss him terribly."* I look up and see silent tears running down Mary's face, too.

"It's so hard, Mary."
"I know it, Linda, but for the first time I feel you're going to make it."

Somewhere during the day breakfast got made, the clothes got packed, dishes got washed. I talked again all day and don't remember what I said. I do remember an incredible relief of tension. I recall Mary saying that it was a *do or die* weekend, that she had known that if she couldn't help me this weekend, she would not be able to help at all. That's why she had been pushing professional counseling.

I said it was so hard to use the words, *"Lee is dead."* I remarked how incredibly difficult it had been to say those three words. Mary looked at me and said, "I've got three words to say, too."
"What?"
"Thank you, God. I don't pray all that often, but I prayed for you last night. I just want to give credit where it's due."

I put my head in my hands and look at the floor. It is so mind-boggling, so intense and so personal that I don't know how to deal with it. I am so moved that inside me, another wall crumbles.

I look at Mary and say, *"Thank you, too."*
"None needed."
"I need to say it."
I wonder if she will ever know what she has done for me.

October 22nd

I feel that somehow and in some way, I have reached deep inside myself and come up with handfuls of me that I didn't know existed. I have an awareness of parts of me that weren't there before. It is difficult to sort out the feelings I have because it is something I have never experienced before. I have no name to attach to it.

I found things inside me that I don't like–selfishness, manipulation, weakness, lies, a spoiled child in a woman's role, not giving, not thinking, not reasoning. I found myself lacking in gratitude and wanting to be repaid for everything I'd ever done for anyone. I found myself lying, not only to others but to myself. I realize that I had been using *strong* as a way of running from the truth, the greatest weakness of all. I was forced to realize it, verbalize it. By doing so, I have gotten in touch with something I should have never lost.

I've felt that if I showed anything it would be interpreted as a sign of weakness and vanity would not allow me to be weak. It's not the outer shell that counts, it's what's inside. My shell was holding in anger, pain and bitterness. It kept out the light, so that healing could not occur.

My shell probably kept out the help that was offered and the support that was rejected. I would not accept needing help. I know now that what I needed was not a tough shell but a strong core. Something, a frame perhaps, that could hold and support the wounded parts until they could mend, something that would allow the pain to surface and be soothed and finally dissipate. Instead, I kept my pain inside and allowed it to ricochet back and forth, never dealing with it and never letting it go. I only dodged it as it bounced back and forth inside me. At the same time I was proud of my ability to cope when in fact I was only denying reality. It's a humbling admission.

I have said before that Lee is dead. I did not hear or believe it or admit it. I could have said that strawberries are purple or cars are made of bread sticks. I said the words, but they were only words. I'm not sure if I was playing a martyr's role. I've never thought of Joan of Arc as my style, but maybe I've been doing just that. There was something very powerful in Mary's voice. Her questions were unyielding, and I'm sure she felt cruel. Even when the tears were coming and the sobs and the disintegration started, I knew that the questions were the tools she was using to chisel away the shell, to pry open the stainless steel, to break down the walls.

I think sometimes I require constant reassurance that I am somebody of worth. I think I over analyze everything because I don't believe or accept the idea that people could think I'm any good. I'm ashamed to say that there were times when I manipulated people in order to get them to feed my ego. It's embarrassing to realize how superficial I am and how shallow I've been. I realize how much I cover up who I really am in order to satisfy what I think other peoples' expectations are. Mary was a catalyst for an emotional rebirth. I looked at myself honestly and I feel an incredible tranquility.

I do not expect that the pain is over. It may never be over. I do not expect that by some miraculous event I will not cry again or hurt again or feel the anguish of Lee's death. To do so would mean that I had to erase him completely. I don't ever want to do that. Lee is dead and I am alive. I cannot take over his death for him any more than I could take over his life. I pray that his dying was quick and that he did not suffer. I cannot make his death my life.

I woke today thinking of the phrase, "valley of the shadow of death." I'm not a religious person, if there is such a thing, but it's a phrase that has taken on new meaning for me. I feel that indeed I have been walking in a very deep valley, darkened by the shadow of Lee's death. It's suddenly a very apt phrase. I don't know what I believe in the context of God or religion. I do know that I am, at least for now, not consumed by the anger and bitterness toward God that I have felt. I do not understand what occurred this weekend, but it has had some kind of very powerful impact for me. I do not feel that I am fighting within myself. I feel peace and acceptance of reality. I feel calm. I feel some source of certainty and conviction that finally I may be able to recover—not the same as I was. I really don't want to be. Perhaps a newer me, more accepting, less anxious, less doubting, more honest. I'm stronger in a sense, not with the brittle shine of stainless steel but perhaps like an aged, weathered statue, pitted here and there with scratches and dents, yet still standing. I'm honestly being who I am, not pretending to be what I think people expect.

There has been some kind of change in my head. In some way I feel like I've been at crossroads and I've chosen the right path. I have a map now. I think it's time to start the trip. All at once, I'm not afraid of this journey. I know I'll get lost occasionally, but somewhere inside me is the feeling that even if I do, I will not be alone and I will find my way back. I may be tired, hungry and wounded, but I will survive and heal.

When Mary told me she had prayed for me it broke me up. I don't know her beliefs. Her voice shook and her eyes filled with tears. The intensity of it had a profound impact on me. I don't know that I have ever felt what I felt then. I couldn't look at her and I think she worried that she had offended me. In the past six months there have been several people who have said, "I pray for you," and I have resented it. I have resented them for thinking that their voices to a God I was hating would help me. I asked what Mary had prayed for. "Guidance and direction to help you," she said. I was struck by the selflessness of it. "I'm not trying to convert you," she had added. In a sense there was some kind of conversion, not necessarily religious. I'm far from that level. There is instead an acceptance of the possibility that someday I will also sort out my beliefs. I will allow myself to explore them sometime in the future.

It's also very intimidating to realize that for all this time, *I did not see* what I was doing. What seems so clearly obvious now was totally unseen previously. I remember Mary telling me, but I wasn't ready to hear it. It's embarrassing to admit that I was so blind. What makes it doubly humiliating is the fact that I'm a nurse. I've dealt with death and dying. I've taught classes on the stages of grief. I've read it and researched it. I've used the information to intellectualize it so that I didn't feel it. Knowledge helped me to deny.

October 23rd

• •

I called in sick today. I'm still having an emotional rebound from the weekend. It's not an up-and-down thing, but a strange sense of tranquility. It's an odd contrast because it is coupled with a strong sense of purpose. I know there is one thing I have to do, must do, today.

I go downstairs and begin to clean. I rearrange furniture, shoving sofas from one end of the room to the other. I dust and polish, chase cobwebs, vacuum. I make empty places, planning for a new arrangement.

I go into Lee's room and begin. I move the stereo he bought out into the family room. I disassemble the bed and carry the pieces upstairs. I empty dresser drawers. I am emptying the room to the bare walls, not angrily or frantically, but as a rational thing to do.

The computer desk stays here, there is no other spot. The bumper pool table moves in, cues stacked in the corner. I fill the dresser drawers with cards, poker chips, games. I hang pictures and vacuum. It's not Lee's room anymore. It's the game room. The last thing I do is take Lee's name off the wall. The outline of the letters remain, paint faded around them. I hang a cribbage board to cover it.

I throw out some things. I put shirts in Curt's drawer. I end up with a box of small reminders that I need to go through and sort. I am physically exhausted, yet relieved. It is done. It is a confirmation of a commitment to reality. I am sad and I cry a little, but it is done, as it needed to be.

I wash up and drive to the mall. I search all the stores until I find it. I buy it. It's a large empty vase in the shape of a seashell. I buy potting soil and ivy. I cannot fill it with cut flowers that will die and I cannot fill it with anything artificial. I go home and plant the ivy in the shell and deliver it to Mary with a note that reads, "This shell was empty, now it's growing things. Thank you for showing me that it is possible."

October 24th

• •

The patients I recognize look fine. A little frailer, a little more worn, but fine. The staff seems genuinely pleased to see me. I look around this place where I used to work before my promotion and wonder how I ever thought it was big and frightening. I think of the long hours I spent here. I remember the fear and frustration of constant stress. I loved it and yet I would not, could not, return to it. I wonder if I have grown or shrunk, so that this place, one the biggest part of my life, seems so much different.

I stop by Mary's office to get her. My nurse's cap is sitting on top of her file cabinet. I tell her to throw it out. She just smiles.

We go for coffee, sit and talk a little. Larry walks in, surprising us both. We joke a little, a comfortable teasing.

Mary's car is in for repairs and I offer to take her to pick it up after work. About halfway there it dawns on me that Lee's accident occurred directly in front of the garage we are going to. Mary realizes it about three blocks away.

"I'm sorry, Linda. I didn't think."

"No problem. There are lots of firsts, Mary. I haven't been down this street before. I'm OK."

I drop her off and pull out onto the street. I accelerate quickly, wanting to get away from that place. I feel tears starting. It's such a useless place to die. It's such a useless death. I go home and go to bed and before I fall asleep, I once again see the headlights coming at me. What did he feel? Oh my God, what did he feel?

November 4th

● ●

There are times when I have a very pronounced sense of impending disaster. I can't seem to identify the source or the real cause. I frequently feel that I am pacing, caged, waiting for something to happen. At those times, I'm irritable, snappish, short tempered. I find myself angry, mostly at myself, for no reason I know of. I wonder if this is the beginning of the *anger* phase that people keep asking me about. It is a tiring experience!

Other times I feel at peace. I can get back into the sensations and feelings I had during the weekend at the lake. Mary and I have talked about it. I still seem to have a sense of importance regarding not only what occurred in my head, but also what real friendship means. Right now, I feel as if I am waiting, maybe for the next phase, maybe for nothing. I hate waiting. I'm impatient, I want to get this over with. I wish I knew what comes next. My crystal ball isn't working.

I turn the pages of my journal and see I haven't written for a while. I'm not sure why. Maybe I'm avoiding the issue. Maybe there's nothing to say. The pain is still there, at times just as intense, at other times, aching. I am wounded by the little things. The big things like the holidays, I have avoided thinking about even getting through them.

I do notice some changes, though. I can talk about Lee with a little more equilibrium. My talk is not always followed by tears now, just incredible sadness.

The tears are still there; sometimes at night, sometimes when I'm alone, sometimes in the car, but I don't cry as often. Sad way to measure progress.

I know this journal is not complete. I have not written about the accident or the hospital or many things about the funeral. They are clear images in my mind, photographically sharp, vivid, painful, real. I cannot yet think about them enough to write and describe them. That in itself is contradictory to the truth. I very frequently think about all that, yet I am unable to write them. There is something about putting words on paper that makes things more real. I am, after all is said and done, after my rebirth weekend, still denying. Maybe the word isn't really denying. I know, accept and acknowledge the fact that Lee is dead. I also know, accept and acknowledge the fact that sometimes I want to avoid the hurt. I don't know if that's a sign of intelligence or cowardice.

February 18th

● ●

I get home from work, change my clothes and sit down to read the paper. In the obituaries a familiar name jumps out at me. The father of a young man I once worked with has died at the age of 56. Craig, the son, was a bookkeeper. We'd joked and laughed together at the chaos of the day-to-day routine, played silly tricks on each other, and become friends. It was unlikely bonding; he was 23 and single, me 30, married with three children. We'd gone on to different jobs. Craig is now in Florida with a big corporation. There had been no contact between us for the past two years.

I feel compelled to go to the funeral home. I get dressed again and drive there. I see Craig talking to a man. I stand back until he is free, hoping I am not intruding and yet remembering how much it meant to me when people came. Suddenly, Craig sees me standing there and I know I was right to come. He is walking toward me, arms outstretched, unflinching eye contact for fifty feet. I am enveloped in an embrace, tight bear hug that lasts a long time. In a very soft voice in my ear, I hear him say, "I heard about your son. I didn't know what to say, so I wimped out and didn't do anything and now you're here for me." I am stunned. I didn't come to cause him guilt.

We talk for awhile about our current jobs, our current lives, our current pain. He ignores the others and walks me to the door, arm around my waist, an incredible feeling of closeness. At the door we share another hug and a soft kiss on the cheek. I wonder if I will ever see him again.

I'm at work Friday when Craig calls. He asks if I'm busy on Saturday for lunch and we make plans to meet.

At lunch we sit and talk about a lot of things. Conversation turns to the loss of his dad, pain still raw. I try to give him what I've learned. I try to give him a chance to say what he needs to say. I try to give him the pitfalls to avoid while he negotiates his own maze of grief. I feel an intense desire to communicate more to him. I can't, and I'm saddened by my failure.

We realize we've been sitting there for 3 hours. It's time to leave. I thank him for lunch. "I realize you have a lot of things to do and people you need to see. You took a long time with me." He looks at me for a moment and softly says, "You never let me be comfortable. You always made me look at the alternatives for my own good. You made me think, and you are my friend."

The Beginning and the End
ℐpril 19th*

• •

The four of us are sitting in the living room. Mary, Larry, Ted and I, friends who spend evenings talking and laughing, teasing each other, enjoying each other's presence. We argue, in good nature, familiar themes now cues for the others to jump in; women's lib, country music, fishing versus expensive vacations, bad jokes, silly puns. We are comfortable together.

Mary wants more snacks. She and I decide to drive to the neighborhood convenience store to get some. The guys add their own list of goodies to buy.

I wait in the car while Mary goes into the store. The fire station is two doors down the street. I hear sirens and tell Mary to watch out for the volunteer firemen. They drive like maniacs to the station, blue lights flashing, whenever the siren sounds.

We pull up in front of my house. My car is gone. I am puzzled. We walk into the living room. There is no one there. Ted and Larry are gone. It's 10:25 p.m. Curt is in the basement watching TV. He has no idea where they are. I still hear sirens. There is a fresh, full glass sitting on the end of the piano near where Larry was sitting.

I walk into the kitchen. There is a new glass, just poured near the phone. I have a sensation of something wrong. Ted and Larry would not just leave. There is no reason. Foreboding. Fear.

We had taken Larry's car and I tell Mary to call her house to check. She does and her kids are fine. Somewhere, deep inside me, I know something is terribly wrong. I know it's mine. The sirens continue their screaming.

I hear a car in the driveway. The front door is thrown open, slamming against the side of the house. I hear Ted yelling at me, "Come on, come on!" I'm asking questions. "What's wrong?" I've never heard Ted's voice like this before, screaming, raw. I hear the word,

(written February 10th)

"accident." Running, grabbing for shoes, leaving my purse, I slide into the front seat of the car. I see Mary standing at the front door. I scream out, "Stay with Curt!" I see her grab Curt as he runs toward us. The sirens haven't stopped.

Larry is driving my car. I'm confused. I'm terrified. I'm deadly sure something horrible has happened. Ted is holding me. I am doubled over with his arms around me. He is saying over and over, "He's going to be all right. He's going to be all right." I feel hysteria creeping in. I'm starting to cry. I'm shaking. I ask, " What is he doing? Is he conscious? How bad is he?"

In a too calm, too flat, too quiet voice, I hear Larry say, "It's a bad accident, Linda." There is a warning inside me. The voice is not Larry's. The tone is all wrong. I hear Ted say, "He's going to be all right. They're working on him. They're pushing on his chest."

In that one hideous, horrible instant time stops and I know. Eighteen year-old boys don't need CPR. I know. Oh, my God, I know! Oh, my God. No!

There is a sensation inside me, a sudden halt of everything. It's as though a shade is coming down in front of me. I am suddenly aware of being absolutely calm, deadly calm, feel-nothing calm.

We are not at the hospital yet. It is 10:30 p.m. on Saturday night, in a car driving too fast and moving too slow. I know my son is dead.

10:45 p.m.
● ●

Ted and Larry jump out of the car, running toward the emergency room. I am running in my brain, but my legs won't work. I can't keep up. They don't look back. I see ambulances parked there, sense men standing near.

I walk to a window. There is a woman behind it. I ask her for information. "They just brought my son in, Lee Musser, car accident, 18 years-old, blond." She looks straight at me and says, *"No, we don't have any one by that name here."*

I am confused. I walk to where I think I'll find Ted and Larry, the waiting room area. They are not there. I glance out the door to the entrance and see both of them walking out of the building. Ted is punching a brick wall with his fist and Larry has his arm tightly around Ted's shoulders trying to talk to him. They are spotlighted by the entrance signs, walking away from me into the darkness. I follow, but they are gone.

I turn back into the emergency room waiting area and sit down. A strange man walks up to me and calls me by name. He is tall, with salt and pepper grey hair with thin blue jeans. He says he is a para-medic, the one who brought Lee in. He says they are working on him. He says no one has time to talk to me, they are busy helping Lee. He is using the therapeutic tone-to-the-hysterical-person voice, dropped an octave, measured, calming. He is kneeling in front of me, never breaking eye contact, never blinking. He tells me they will let me know the minute they have time. He tells me to relax, that Lee is being taken care of, that they are doing everything they can. I believe him. I ask his name. He ignores the question.

Time passes. I go to the window again. I'm asking the same face-less woman for information. I say, "I'm not trying to be a hysterical mother, but I have to know!" I hear my voice rising.

She begins asking questions.
"Name?"
"Lee Michael Musser. M-u-s-s-e-r."
"Address?" She appears bored.
"6860 Harrison."
"Insurance?"
"Yes."
"What kind? Policy number?" Routine questions, routine shift.
"I have no idea." I can feel the control ebbing, my voice is getting shrill.
"Social Security Number?" She turns to someone behind the win-dow and asks if the coffee is ready. She turns back and repeats, "Social Security Number?"

I'm losing control! I have no idea what Lee's Social Security Number is. My hands press down on the counter in front of me. I feel myself getting taller.

Suddenly, Larry is there. I hear him tell her that he will give her all the information she needs. I am so thankful for his taking charge. I hear an edge in his voice, a firmness, a close-to-anger tone. I wonder if he knows Lee's Social Security Number. I have to get hold of myself.

I turn around and am directed to a little office. It is very small, very narrow, my feet could touch the opposite wall if I extended my legs.

Larry appears with coffee. Ted, Larry and I sit, saying nothing. A policeman comes in and asks us about car insurance, tells us about accident reports to be given to insurance agents.

A familiar face appears in the doorway. Martha is my next-door neighbor who works at the hospital. She is leaving work and has seen us sitting there. She knows Lee. He's cut her grass and played with her dogs. He talks to her. Just last week he went over to tell her about his new stereo. She asks what we're doing here and we tell her it's Lee. We tell her we know nothing.

She disappears through the double doors. I feel better knowing she is with him. He is no longer just another accident to them. Martha is there. She will tell them she knows him. He will become *Someone.*

11:30 p.m.

We still sit in this small room, lights glaring, silent except for occasional words, "Not Lee." A security guard comes in and tells us to try to rest. It's going to be a long night. Larry leaves and returns several times. I tell him where Michelle is so Mary can find her if she needs to.

It seems we have been here for weeks. I am sure it is probably less than an hour. Martha is in and out, at one point taking me to a bathroom when I say I am nauseated. I run water on my wrists and wipe my face. I say I just needed to get away. She says, "It's okay, we can all see what you're trying to do." I have no idea what she means.

We sit, Ted and I, side by side, facing a blank wall. Ted stares straight ahead, every now and then saying, "Not Lee." He is crying, not trying to hide it.

I am not crying. I am trying to prepare Ted for what will come next. I am a nurse. I know the routine. I am holding his hand and wiping the tears from his face. Larry sits, head down. He is there, comforting in his presence. We are drawing strength-by-association from him.

After a long time the door opens and Martha is standing there. She has the same look in her eyes. Before she says anything, before she has to try to put it into words, very softly, from the depths of my soul, comes a whispering moan, "No Martha." I am slowly shaking my head. Just as slowly, she, with tears in her eyes shakes her head, too.

I look away. Larry is kneeling. His eyes meet mine and I see pain and shock. He is hurting for us. We become a slow-motion movie. There is a long, frozen time where we stare at each other. Then slowly, centimeters at a time, his head drops, eyes to the floor. He whispers, "Oh, my God." I turn to Ted and we hold each other. Our son is dead.

12:30 a.m.

L arry softly asks if I want him to go stay with the kids and have Mary here with me. I nod. I don't want to hurt his feelings. I hope he understands. He asks if I want them to tell Michelle and Curt. I say, "No." I must tell them myself. I must be there when they hear it. I can't imagine the words I will use.

There is a steady parade of people, now, in and out of this glaring little room. Each one says they are sorry. Each one looks awkward. Each one has a job to do. A policeman apologetically says there is a problem with Lee's driver's license. It doesn't show up on the computer. In a very tired voice I state flatly, "He has a valid driver's license." I have no idea why I think he will believe me against the computer. As he leaves he seems to fill the room, maroon and grey uniform, handcuffs clanking. I wonder what he is thinking.

Martha comes in. I ask her if there is any possibility of organ dona-
tion. She says, " No. He's been too long without oxygen." I am saddened. It would have at least helped someone else.

Martha asks about funeral homes. I don't even remember the
names of any. Ted suggests a new place nearby. A friend of ours
built it. I feel it is right.

I look at Martha and say, "They don't have to do an autopsy, do
they?" My voice sounds funny – pleading, wistful, small. Martha
looks at me sadly and says, "Yes. It's a coroner's case." I nod slowly and say, "I know." I am wishing they could just leave him alone,
yet I know the rules. I try not to think about it.

I look at Martha and say, "I have to see him." "You don't want to see
him now, Linda. He's still got his tubes in and everything." I shake
my head and in a very controlled, calm, determined voice I hear
myself say, "I *have* to see him, Martha." Our eyes meet. She disappears behind the double doors.

Now Mary is here. She is quiet. I feel better knowing she is with us.
I am not interacting with her. I am just comforted by her presence.

Martha returns and says we can go in now if we're sure we want
to. There is no doubt in my mind. I must see him.

We walk through the double doors and I am conscious of people
standing in the doorway watching me. Someone is holding my arm,
guiding me. He has a stethoscope around his neck. I hear someone call him, Doctor.

There is a door ahead of me. Slowly, I walk into the room. There is
shiny yellow tile, equipment silent, monitors with no beeping, oxygen with no hiss. It is totally still.

There is a stretcher in the center of the room. I am amazed at how
big he is. He seems to be sleeping. He is wearing a shirt I hate. He
should have died with better clothes on. I walk to his side and put
my hand on his chest. He is warm and still. There is a tiny cut on
his temple, a small drop of blood trickling down into his hair. I must

get a Band-aid for that. I stare at his face. He missed a spot shaving this morning. There is a little bruise on his eyelid. I need to get ice on it or his eye will be black tomorrow.

Ted is running his fingers through Lee's hair. I hear him talking, but I can't make out the words. Time is standing still. I know this moment will be engraved on my brain forever.

I very slowly look up from my son's face to see Mary and Martha in the doorway. I have never seen that expression before on people's faces. I meet Mary's eyes. I feel my eyes are open very wide. We stare at each other and I see sadness and pain and death in her soul. I have no idea what she sees in mine.

There is pressure on my elbow. The man is saying that it is time to go. I allow myself to be led away from Lee. I don't want to go; yet I do not resist. Martha and Mary are leading Ted, the doctor has me. The same people are in the same doorways. The same silence is there as we pass. Everything is frozen and timeless and still, yet I keep moving.

We are back in our tiny, glaring room. Mary disappears for a minute. When she returns, she has a towel in her hands. She walks over to Ted. Ted extends his hands together, palms up. I watch as my best friend slowly, tenderly washes my son's blood from my husbands hands.

To All The People Who Loved Lee

By his Mother – Read at Lee's funeral

We would like very much to talk to each of you and say the things we feel right now. We have asked ourselves, *"Why?"* a hundred times and we have no answers. Maybe we never will. A terrible tragedy has occurred and Lee is gone. We wonder why a life so short has to end, but we hope that all of us can concentrate on the things Lee did and not the things he didn't have time to do.

Lee was loved and he loved in return. He laughed and made others laugh with him. He was intelligent and bright. He made plans for the future and worked to make them a reality. He played not one, but two musical instruments. He could make a jumble of wires, a TV set and a computer do incredible things. He knew CPR. He held a job and went to school. He was accepted at Purdue University. He participated in and won awards at state and local band and orchestra contests. He had friends who cared, really cared, about him. He developed and operated his own computer bulletin board service. He swam. He donated blood. He played chess. He was interested in astronomy and helped at the planetarium. He earned the respect of his teachers. There are many, many people who don't accomplish that much in 50 or 60 years of life. We can be proud of what he did.

We have many things to be grateful for: Lee's friends, Mike, Carlin, Jess, Ceasar, George, Vakis, Dave and all the others. They shared Lee's life and became part of our family.

We are thankful for the very special teachers that Lee knew: Ms. Dunscomb, Ms. Williams, Mr. Stolting, Mr. Gregg Williams and all the others who helped Lee explore the world and set his sights on college and learning all he could.

We are thankful for the wonderful, compassionate friends: Mary and Larry Gilbert, Dolly and Marty Snemis, Wendy Swisher and all the rest. They will never know how much they have helped us during this terrible time.

We are thankful for our family who has shared our grief as well as our joys. We are thankful that our son, in his 18 years, somehow positively touched the lives of each one of the people who have been here in the past two days.

No one is ever really gone as long as someone remembers him, so please remember Lee. But when you do, remember the laughter, not the tears. Remember the jokes and his sense of humor, not sadness. Remember the giving, caring, happy, young man who was, not what might have been.

Thank you all for your kindness, but most of all, thank you for loving Lee, and let this day be not a memory of his death, but a celebration of his life.

With our deepest thanks and love, Ted, Linda, Michelle and Curt

Linda Leith Musser is a registered nurse who is currently employed as Vice President of Patient Services at Porter Memorial Hospital in Valparaiso, Indiana. She has worked in many health care areas, including long-term care and staff education, as well as teaching both undergraduate and graduate courses at the Valparaiso University College of Nursing. Ms. Musser completed her Baccalaureate Degree in Nursing at the University of Evansville in Evansville, Indiana. She received her Masters Degree in Nursing Administration from Indiana University School of Nursing in Indianapolis, Indiana and is currently completing the requirements for her Doctoral.

• •

Ms. Musser is the mother of two children, Michelle and Curtis.
Her eldest son, Lee, was killed in an automobile accident in 1986.